PIANO · VOCAL · GUITAR

VANESSA CARLT[ON]

RABBITS ON THE RUN

ISBN 978-1-4584-0540-1

HAL•LEONARD®
CORPORATION

7777 W. BLUEMOUND RD. P.O. BOX 13819 MILWAUKEE, WI 53213

Rabbits on the Run is a collaboration between myself, Steve Osborne,
Patrick Hallahan of My Morning Jacket, Ari Ingber of The Upwelling,
a 1/2 inch tape machine, and a stone house in the English countryside.
This album is inspired by two books: Richard Adams' *Watership Down* and
Stephen Hawking's *A Brief History of Time*. It was written and arranged
over two years and put on tape at Real World Studios in Box, England.

Transcribing the album into a songbook was a wonderful process and a
rare treat for me as a pianist. Many of the editing sessions took place via
speaker phone; one phone resting on top of my piano in New York City
and one phone on Dan Geisler's piano in Colorado. Our job was to take
the instrumental and vocal melodies from the album and boil them down
into one arrangement for the piano. We were careful to maintain the vibe
of each song and our hope is that each transcription stands on its own as
a dynamic piece of sheet music.

I dedicate this book to Heidi Carlton and her students.

Special thanks to Dan Geisler, Jeff Radke, Jordan Feldstein,
Universal Publishing, and Hal Leonard.

Best

CAROUSEL

Words and Music by
VANESSA CARLTON

I DON'T WANT TO BE A BRIDE

Music by VANESSA CARLTON,
ARI INGBER and STEVE OSBORNE
Words by VANESSA CARLTON

Lyrics: I like your com-pa-ny. You've got a fresh phi-los - o-phy, nev-er knew such a gen-tle-man.

LONDON

Words and Music by
VANESSA CARLTON

FAIR WEATHER FRIENDS

Words and Music by
VANESSA CARLTON

mag - i - cal ___ think - ing ___ gets ___ us ___ by. ___

My fair -

HEAR THE BELLS

Words and Music by
VANESSA CARLTON

DEAR CALIFORNIA

Music by VANESSA CARLTON
and ARI INGBER
Words by VANESSA CARLTON

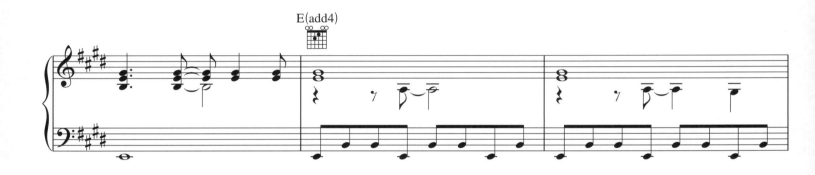

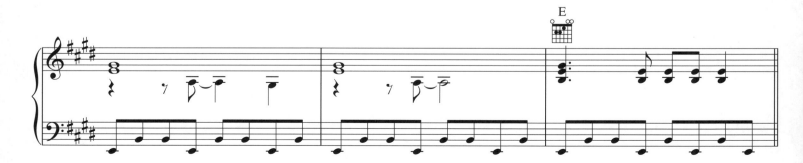

TALL TALES FOR SPRING

Words and Music by
VANESSA CARLTON

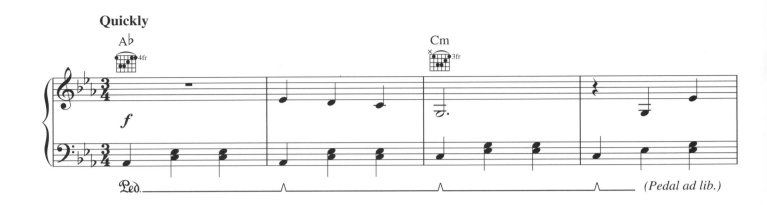

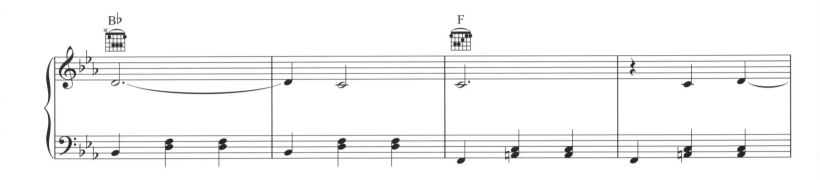

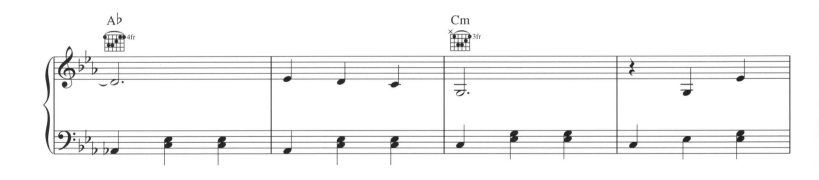

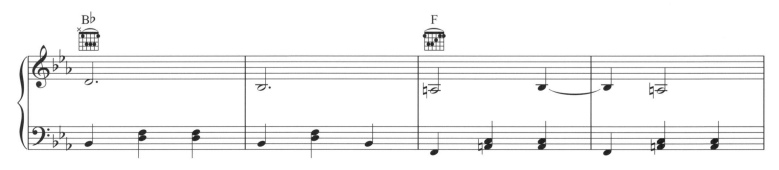

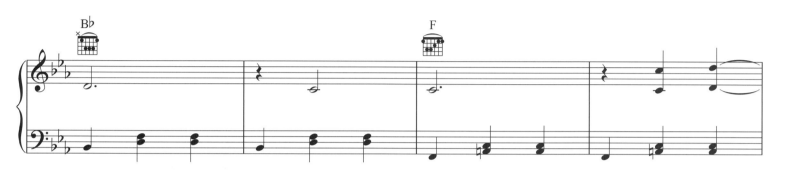

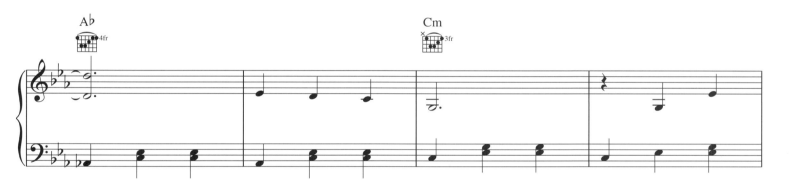

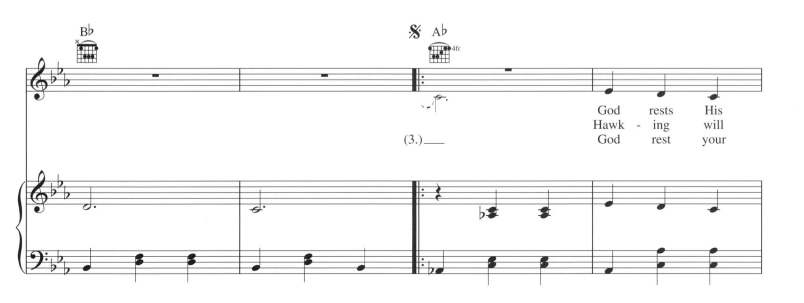

God   rests   His
Hawk - ing   will
God   rest   your

(3.) ___

GET GOOD

Words and Music by
VANESSA CARLTON

A E Bm D

what you mean.___ I want to thank___ you for be-ing so___

A E Bm A

___ good to me.___ I just want-ed you___ to know.___

E A

___ Are the ech-oes com-ing back___ to you? Is

G D

wis-dom see-ing pat-terns on a loom___ like a blan-ket a-round you?___

THE MARCHING LINE

Words and Music by
VANESSA CARLTON

Boots on con - crete don't slip on the leaves.

Smile at the stran - gers who know what you mean.

*Lead vocal written an octave higher than sung.

IN THE END

Words and Music by
VANESSA CARLTON

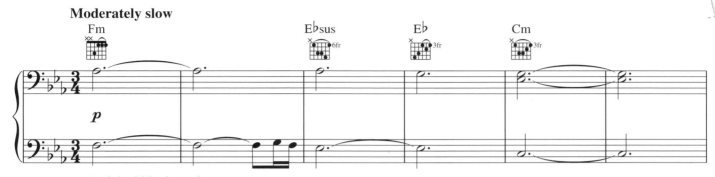

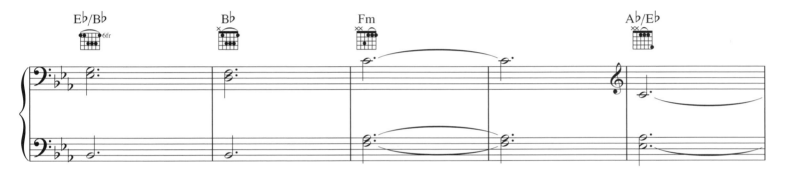

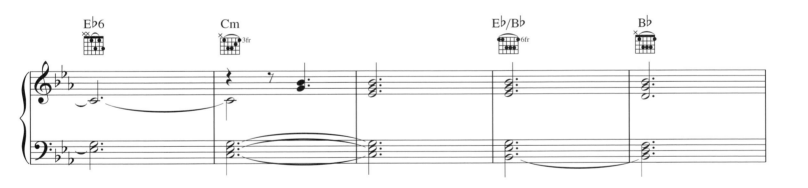

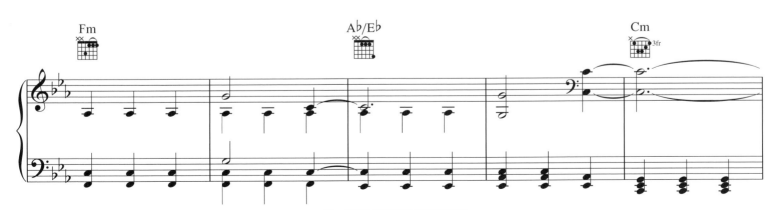

Lyrics:
And in the end, ___ we be-gin a-gain. ___ It's ___ the way of all things. ___ Your